Helen Keller

by
DAVID A. ADLER
illustrated by
JOHN WALLNER

Holiday House / New York

For Jonathan and Leah,
Shana, David, and Shira
D. A. A.

For the rebellious spirit
waiting with beating heart
for something to happen
J. C. W.

First Edition

Library of Congress Cataloging-in-Publication Data

Adler, David A.
Helen Keller / by David A. Adler ; illustrated by John Wallner.—1st ed.
p. cm.
Summary: A brief biography highlights some of the struggles and
accomplishments in the life of Helen Keller.
Includes bibliographical references.
ISBN 0-8234-1606-2 (hardcover)
1. Keller, Helen, 1880–1968—Juvenile literature. 2. Blind-deaf women—
United States—Biography—Juvenile literature. 3. Blind-deaf—United States—
Biography—Juvenile literature. 4. Sullivan, Annie, 1866–1936—Juvenile literature.
[I. Keller, Helen, 1880–1968. 2. Blind. 3. Deaf. 4. People with disabilities.
5.Women—biography. 6. Sullivan, Annie, 1866–1936.]
I. Wallner, John C., ill. II. Title.
HV1624.K4 A448 2003
362.4′1′092—dc21
[B]   2002027580

Contents

1. Illness

Helen Keller was a writer
and speaker.
She was a friend of presidents.
Helen Keller was deaf and blind.
Still she was one
of the great women
of her time.

Helen Keller

was born on June 27, 1880.

She was born in a small

town in Alabama.

She was a beautiful baby,

and she was smart.

At six months old,

she began talking.

On her first birthday,

she began walking.

But then, a few months
before her second birthday,
Helen became ill.
The doctor thought she would die.

Helen lived,
but she lost her sight and hearing.
After that, the world for her
was dark and silent.

2. From Darkness into Light

Helen Keller did not hear
people speak, so she did not
learn new words.
Soon she forgot the few words
she already knew.
Helen had her own way of talking.
When she pushed someone away,
she meant "Go."
When she pulled someone,
she meant "Come."
When Helen pretended
to put on eyeglasses,
she meant "Father."

Helen Keller had
about sixty such signs.
Still, there were many things
she wanted to say, but could not.
Sometimes Helen touched
people's lips.

When their lips moved,
she knew they were talking.
But she didn't know
what they were saying.
Helen moved *her* lips.
She waved her hands.
But she knew she wasn't speaking.

"This made me so angry,"
Helen wrote later,
"that I kicked and screamed."
Her parents took her to doctors.
But nothing could be done
to help Helen see and hear.
Next the Kellers looked for
a teacher for Helen.

They went to Washington, D.C.,
to Alexander Graham Bell.
He had invented the telephone.
Dr. Bell had once been a teacher
in a school for the deaf.

"He understood my signs,"
Helen wrote later.
"I knew it and
loved him at once."
Dr. Bell helped find a teacher
for Helen.

3. That Living Word

"The most important day
in all my life," Helen wrote later,
"is the one on which my teacher,
Anne Mansfield Sullivan,
came to me."
The day was March 3, 1887.
Helen was six years old.

For Helen's first lesson,
Anne used the finger alphabet.
She spelled *d-o-l-l* in Helen's hand.
Then she gave Helen a doll.
For Helen, this was a game.

She did not know that
what was spelled in her
hand was a doll.
She did not know that
everything had a name.

One day, while taking a walk,
Anne and Helen came to a
water pump.
Anne put one of Helen's hands
in the water.
In Helen's other hand,
Anne spelled *w-a-t-e-r*.
Suddenly Helen knew
what Anne was trying to teach her.

Everything has a name.

Helen learned many new words
that day.

That night, for the first time,
Helen Keller "longed for a new day
to come."

4. Hope and Love

Helen learned hundreds,
then thousands of words.
She learned to talk and hear
with her hands.

She learned to read by feeling

tiny bumps on paper.

That kind of writing for the blind

is called Braille.

When Helen was ten,

she learned to speak.

She could not hear the sounds

she or others made.

She never learned to speak clearly.

In 1900, Helen went to
Radcliffe College.
Anne Sullivan sat next to her.
She spelled in Helen's hand
what was said in class.
While Helen was in college,
she wrote *The Story of My Life*.
People all over the world read it.

Later Helen wrote other books.
She went across the United States.
Thousands of people came to hear
her speak.

She went to Europe and Japan, too.

Helen marched for women's rights.

She wrote about the many needs
of working people and the poor.

During and after
the Second World War,
Helen visited soldiers
made blind and deaf in the war.
Helen gave them hope
that they, too, would live
full and happy lives.

Helen Keller said
she was happy because
she had good friends and
interesting work to do.

In 1964, for her good work,
President Lyndon Johnson gave her
the Presidential Medal of Freedom.

Helen Keller died on June 1, 1968.
People everywhere cried
for her.
A world of people she could not see
and could not hear had loved her.
And Helen Keller had loved them.

Important Dates

June 27, 1880

Helen Keller is born in Tuscumbia, Alabama.

February 1882

As a result of an illness,
she becomes blind and deaf.

March 1887

She meets Anne Sullivan.

1900

She becomes a student at Radcliffe College.
She begins her work for the American
Foundation for the Blind.

October 20, 1936

Anne Sullivan dies.

1964

Helen Keller is awarded the
Presidential Medal of Freedom.

June 1, 1968

Helen Keller dies.

Sources

Keller, Helen. *The Story of My Life*. New York: Doubleday, 1954.

Keller, Helen. *Midstream: My Later Life*. New York: Greenwood Press, 1968.

Lash, Joseph P. *Helen and Teacher: The Story of Helen Keller and Anne Sullivan Macy*. New York: Delacorte, 1980.